Disclaimer: The information provided in this book is for educational and informational purposes only and should not be considered as a substitute for medical advice, diagnosis, or treatment. It is not intended to replace the advice of healthcare professionals or addiction specialists. The author and publisher of this book do not assume any liability for the information contained herein, including but not limited to, any errors or omissions, or the consequences of any actions taken based on the information provided. It is recommended that readers consult with their healthcare providers before making any changes to their smoking habits or starting any new treatments or programs.

Introduction: Why Quitting Smoking is Important

Smoking is a dangerous habit that can lead to serious health consequences. It is the leading cause of preventable deaths worldwide, causing an estimated 8 million deaths per year. In addition to causing lung cancer, smoking is associated with a number of other health problems, including heart disease, stroke, respiratory illnesses, and more.

Quitting smoking is crucial for maintaining good health and reducing the risk of these serious health problems. Research has shown that even those who have smoked for years can benefit from quitting. Within just a few hours of quitting smoking, the body starts to experience positive changes, such as improved circulation and reduced levels of carbon monoxide in the blood.

Quitting smoking can also lead to a number of other benefits, such as improved lung function, increased energy levels, and better overall health. It can also help to reduce the risk of other health problems, such as infertility, premature aging, and tooth decay.

In addition to the health benefits, quitting smoking can also improve quality of life in other ways. It can lead to better relationships, increased self-confidence, and a greater sense of control over one's life. Quitting smoking can also save money and free up time that would have been spent smoking or dealing with the consequences of smoking.

Overall, quitting smoking is important for maintaining good health, reducing the risk of serious health problems, and improving quality of life. It's never too late to quit smoking and start reaping the benefits of a smoke-free lifestyle.

Chapter 1: The Dangers of Smoking

Smoking is a dangerous and highly addictive habit that poses numerous health risks. Cigarettes contain thousands of chemicals, many of which are toxic and can cause serious harm to the body. In this chapter, we'll explore the various dangers of smoking, including its effects on the respiratory system, cardiovascular system, and overall health.

First and foremost, smoking is a leading cause of lung cancer, a disease that claims the lives of thousands of people every year. Smoking also increases the risk of other respiratory conditions, such as chronic obstructive pulmonary disease (COPD) and emphysema. These conditions can make it difficult to breathe and lead to chronic coughing, wheezing, and shortness of breath.

Smoking also has a significant impact on the cardiovascular system. It can damage the blood vessels, leading to atherosclerosis (a buildup of plaque in the arteries) and an increased risk of heart attack and stroke. Smoking also contributes to high blood pressure and can cause irregular heart rhythms.

In addition to these specific health risks, smoking can have a negative impact on overall health and wellbeing. It can cause premature aging, including wrinkles and age spots, and can make it more difficult for the body to heal from injuries and illnesses. Smoking also harms the immune system, making it more difficult for the body to fight off infections and diseases.

Overall, the dangers of smoking are clear and significant. Quitting smoking is the best thing you can do for your health and wellbeing, and this book is here to help you on your journey to becoming smoke-free.

Chapter 2: How Smoking Affects Your Health

Smoking is one of the most significant causes of preventable death worldwide. Not only does it increase the risk of lung cancer, but it also affects nearly every organ in the body. In this chapter, we'll take a closer look at how smoking affects your health and why quitting is essential.

First and foremost, smoking damages your lungs. It can cause chronic bronchitis, emphysema, and other respiratory diseases that make it difficult to breathe. Over time, smoking can cause lung cancer, which is the leading cause of cancer death worldwide.

Smoking also affects your heart health. It increases your risk of coronary heart disease, stroke, and other cardiovascular diseases. Nicotine, the addictive substance found in cigarettes, causes your blood vessels to constrict, making it harder for blood to flow. This increased strain on the heart and blood vessels can lead to heart attacks and strokes.

In addition to respiratory and cardiovascular diseases, smoking also affects your digestive system. It increases your risk of developing ulcers, acid reflux, and other gastrointestinal problems. It can also damage your teeth and gums, leading to tooth decay and gum disease.

Smoking also affects your skin and appearance. It can cause premature aging, wrinkles, and skin discoloration. It can also lead to hair loss and other cosmetic issues.

Overall, smoking has a significant impact on your health and well-being. The good news is that quitting smoking can have immediate and long-term health benefits. By quitting smoking, you reduce your risk of developing smoking-related diseases and improve your overall quality of life.

Chapter 3: The Benefits of Quitting Smoking

Quitting smoking is one of the most significant positive changes you can make for your health. While it may be challenging to quit, the benefits of quitting are numerous and will improve your quality of life in many ways.

Improved Health: Smoking is linked to numerous health problems, including lung cancer, heart disease, stroke, and respiratory illnesses such as chronic bronchitis and emphysema. Quitting smoking reduces your risk of these diseases, and your body begins to heal immediately after quitting.

Increased Life Expectancy: Studies have shown that quitting smoking can add years to your life expectancy. According to the American Cancer Society, those who quit smoking before age 50 have a 50% chance of living an additional 10 years, and those who quit before age 40 may add as much as 9 years to their life expectancy.

Better Respiratory Function: Smoking damages the lungs and reduces respiratory function, making it harder to breathe. Quitting smoking can help improve lung function and make it easier to breathe.

Improved Cardiovascular Health: Smoking is a leading cause of heart disease and stroke. Quitting smoking can help lower your blood pressure, reduce your risk of heart disease and stroke, and improve overall cardiovascular health.

Better Quality of Life: Quitting smoking can lead to improved overall health and well-being. You may experience increased energy levels, better sleep, and improved sense of taste and smell.

Financial Savings: Smoking is expensive, and quitting can save you a significant amount of money over time. Not only will you save money by not purchasing cigarettes, but you may also save money on health care costs associated with smoking-related illnesses.

In conclusion, quitting smoking has numerous benefits for your health and well-being. While quitting smoking may be difficult, the benefits of quitting far outweigh the temporary discomfort of nicotine withdrawal. Take the first step towards better health and quit smoking today.

Chapter 4: Understanding Nicotine Addiction

Nicotine is a highly addictive substance found in cigarettes, cigars, and other tobacco products. It is one of the main reasons why people find it so difficult to quit smoking. Nicotine addiction occurs when the brain becomes dependent on nicotine to function normally. In this chapter, we'll explore the science behind nicotine addiction and how it affects the body and mind.

When you inhale smoke from a cigarette, cigar, or other tobacco product, the nicotine in the smoke enters your bloodstream and travels to your brain. Once in the brain, nicotine binds to specific receptors that release a chemical called dopamine. Dopamine is a neurotransmitter that is responsible for feelings of pleasure and reward.

Over time, the brain becomes accustomed to the release of dopamine triggered by nicotine. As a result, the brain begins to crave nicotine to maintain the same levels of pleasure and reward. This is what leads to nicotine addiction.

Nicotine addiction is both physical and psychological. The physical aspect of addiction occurs when the body becomes dependent on nicotine to function normally. Withdrawal symptoms, such as headaches, irritability, and difficulty concentrating, can occur when nicotine levels drop in the body. Psychological addiction occurs when the mind associates smoking with certain activities or emotions, such as stress or socializing.

Understanding the science behind nicotine addiction is an essential first step in quitting smoking. It helps you to recognize that the addiction is not a personal failure, but rather a physical and psychological dependence on nicotine. By understanding the addiction, you can better prepare yourself for the quitting process and develop effective strategies for managing cravings and withdrawal symptoms.

Chapter 5: The Physical Effects of Nicotine Withdrawal

When you quit smoking cigarettes, your body will begin to experience a range of physical symptoms as it adjusts to the absence of nicotine. This process is known as nicotine withdrawal, and it can be one of the most challenging aspects of quitting smoking.

One of the most common physical effects of nicotine withdrawal is the onset of cravings for nicotine. These cravings can be intense and persistent, and they may be accompanied by feelings of irritability, anxiety, and restlessness.

Other physical symptoms of nicotine withdrawal can include headaches, increased appetite, and difficulty concentrating. Some people may also experience gastrointestinal distress, such as nausea, vomiting, or constipation.

While the physical effects of nicotine withdrawal can be uncomfortable, they are generally short-lived and will subside as your body adjusts to life without nicotine. In the meantime, there are a number of strategies that can help manage these symptoms, such as engaging in physical activity, staying hydrated, and practicing relaxation techniques like deep breathing or meditation.

Remember, while nicotine withdrawal can be challenging, it is a normal and expected part of the process of quitting smoking. By staying committed to your goal of becoming smoke-free, and by utilizing the tools and resources available to you, you can successfully overcome the physical effects of nicotine withdrawal and achieve long-term success in quitting smoking.

Chapter 6: Dealing with Cravings and Triggers

One of the biggest challenges when quitting smoking is dealing with the cravings and triggers that can lead to relapse. Cravings are the intense urges to smoke that can be triggered by a variety of stimuli, such as stress, social situations, or the sight or smell of cigarettes. Triggers are the environmental, emotional, and social cues that can lead to cravings and make it difficult to resist the urge to smoke.

The first step in dealing with cravings and triggers is to identify them. Keep a journal or record of when cravings occur and what seems to trigger them. This will help you anticipate and prepare for situations that may lead to cravings. For example, if you always crave a cigarette after a meal, you can plan to take a walk or engage in a distracting activity instead.

When a craving does occur, try some of the following strategies to manage it:

Distract yourself: Engage in an activity that requires your full attention, such as reading a book, taking a walk, or listening to music.

Deep breathing: Take a few slow, deep breaths to calm your mind and body.

Delay: Tell yourself you will wait 10 minutes before giving into the craving. Often, cravings will pass within this time frame.

Positive self-talk: Remind yourself of the reasons why you quit smoking and the benefits of being smoke-free.

Seek support: Reach out to a friend or family member for encouragement and support.

It's also important to address triggers by making changes to your environment or habits. For example, if smoking was a part of your morning routine, try switching to a different beverage or activity. If social situations trigger cravings, consider avoiding situations where smoking is present or let your friends and family know that you are quitting smoking and ask for their support.

Finally, be patient with yourself. Quitting smoking is a process, and it's normal to experience cravings and setbacks along the way. Remember that each time you successfully manage a craving or resist a trigger, you are building your skills and confidence in staying smoke-free. With time and practice, you can develop the tools to overcome cravings and triggers and live a healthy, smoke-free life.

Chapter 7: How to Prepare Yourself for Quitting Smoking

Quitting smoking is a challenging process, but with the right preparation, you can increase your chances of success. Here are some steps to take as you prepare to quit smoking:

Set a quit date: Choose a date in the near future and mark it on your calendar. Use this time to prepare yourself mentally and physically for the quitting process.

Identify your triggers: Think about the situations or emotions that typically trigger your desire to smoke, such as stress or social situations. Make a list of these triggers and plan how you will cope with them.

Find a support system: It's essential to have people in your life who can support and encourage you as you quit smoking. This could be friends, family, or a support group.

Develop a plan: Identify the strategies and tools that you will use to help you quit smoking, such as nicotine replacement therapy, counseling, or alternative therapies like acupuncture or hypnosis.

Remove smoking-related items: Get rid of all cigarettes, lighters, ashtrays, and other smoking-related items from your home, car, and workplace. This will help you avoid temptation and reduce the chances of relapse.

Practice stress-reducing techniques: Smoking is often a way to cope with stress, so it's important to find other ways to manage stress during the quitting process. Try techniques like deep breathing, meditation, or yoga to help you stay calm and centered.

Reward yourself: Set up a system of rewards for yourself as you reach milestones in your quitting journey. This could be something as simple as treating yourself to a favorite food or activity.

By taking these steps, you can prepare yourself for quitting smoking and set yourself up for success. Remember that quitting smoking is a process, and it's okay to ask for help and support along the way.

Chapter 8: Choosing a Quit Date

Choosing a quit date is an important step in the process of quitting smoking. It gives you a specific target to work toward and helps you mentally prepare for the change you're about to make. Here are some tips to help you choose a quit date that works for you:

Set a realistic date: Choose a date that is realistic for you to prepare for. Don't rush into quitting without preparing yourself mentally and physically.

Avoid stressful times: Try to avoid quitting during times of stress, such as during a busy work period or during a family crisis. Quitting smoking can be challenging, and it's best to avoid additional stressors that may make it even more difficult.

Plan around triggers: Consider your smoking triggers when choosing a quit date. For example, if you usually smoke more when you're out with friends, it may be best to choose a quit date when you have fewer social engagements.

Use a meaningful date: Choosing a meaningful date, such as a birthday or anniversary, can help motivate you and make your quit date more memorable.

Get support: Let your friends and family know about your quit date and ask for their support. Having a support system can make a big difference in your success.

Remember, the most important thing is to choose a quit date that works for you. Don't be afraid to adjust your date if necessary. The goal is to make a commitment to quit smoking and take the necessary steps to achieve your goal.

Chapter 9: The First Few Days of Quitting Smoking

The first few days after quitting smoking can be challenging, both physically and mentally. Withdrawal symptoms, such as irritability, anxiety, and headaches, are common and can make it difficult to stick to your goal of becoming smoke-free.

One of the best things you can do during this time is to stay busy and distracted. Try taking a walk, listening to music, or engaging in a hobby you enjoy. Keeping your hands busy with something like a stress ball or a fidget toy can also be helpful.

It's important to stay hydrated during this time, as nicotine withdrawal can cause dehydration. Drink plenty of water and other fluids to help flush the toxins from your body.

Cravings are also a significant challenge during the first few days. It can be helpful to have a plan in place for dealing with cravings when they arise. This might include deep breathing exercises, chewing gum, or using nicotine replacement therapy (NRT) products like patches or gum.

It's important to remember that the first few days are just the beginning of your journey. You will likely experience ups and downs along the way, but the benefits of quitting smoking far outweigh the temporary discomfort you may experience. Stay focused on your goal and take it one day at a time. You've got this!

Chapter 10: How to Stay Motivated to Quit

Quitting smoking is a challenging process, and it's not uncommon for individuals to experience setbacks along the way. However, it's essential to stay motivated and focused on your goal of becoming smoke-free. Here are some strategies that can help you stay motivated during your quitting journey:

Set Goals: Setting achievable goals can provide a sense of accomplishment and motivate you to keep going. Start by setting small goals, such as reducing the number of cigarettes you smoke each day or going one day without smoking. As you achieve each goal, set a new one and continue to work towards becoming smoke-free.

Find Support: Having a support system can be a powerful motivator. Reach out to friends, family, or a support group for encouragement and accountability. You can also consider working with a healthcare professional or counselor to provide additional support and guidance.

Remind Yourself Why You're Quitting: Make a list of the reasons why you want to quit smoking and read it whenever you're feeling unmotivated or tempted to smoke. This can help reinforce your commitment to becoming smoke-free and keep you focused on your goals.

Celebrate Your Successes: Celebrate your successes, no matter how small they may seem. Recognize the progress you've made and the positive changes you've experienced since quitting smoking. Treat yourself to something special, such as a favorite meal or activity, to reward yourself for your hard work.

Visualize Your Future Self: Close your eyes and visualize yourself as a non-smoker. Imagine the benefits you'll experience, such as improved health, increased energy, and greater financial freedom. This can help you stay motivated and committed to your goal of becoming smoke-free.

Remember, quitting smoking is a journey, and it's okay to experience setbacks along the way. Stay motivated and focused on your goal of becoming smoke-free, and don't be afraid to seek support when you need it. With time and persistence, you can achieve your goal of living a smoke-free life.

Chapter 11: Coping Strategies for Withdrawal Symptoms

When you quit smoking, you may experience a range of withdrawal symptoms, such as irritability, anxiety, cravings, and difficulty concentrating. These symptoms can be uncomfortable and challenging to manage, but there are several coping strategies that can help you navigate them.

Deep breathing: Deep breathing exercises can help reduce feelings of stress and anxiety. Take a few slow, deep breaths in through your nose and out through your mouth when you feel overwhelmed or anxious.

Exercise: Physical activity can help reduce cravings and improve mood. Go for a walk, jog, or engage in other forms of exercise to help distract yourself from cravings and boost your mood.

Drink water: Drinking water can help flush out the nicotine and other toxins from your system, and help reduce symptoms like headaches and dry mouth.

Practice mindfulness: Mindfulness techniques, such as meditation and yoga, can help reduce stress and improve your ability to focus on the present moment. Try incorporating these techniques into your daily routine to help manage withdrawal symptoms.

Seek support: Reach out to friends, family, or support groups for help and encouragement. You don't have to go through the quitting process alone.

Use nicotine replacement therapy: Nicotine replacement therapy, such as nicotine gum, patches, or lozenges, can help reduce cravings and manage withdrawal symptoms.

Try alternative therapies: Alternative therapies, such as acupuncture and massage, can help reduce stress and promote relaxation, which may help alleviate withdrawal symptoms.

By using these coping strategies, you can help manage the uncomfortable symptoms of nicotine withdrawal and stay on track with your goal of quitting smoking. Remember, withdrawal symptoms are temporary, and they will subside over time as your body adjusts to life without nicotine.

Chapter 12: Creating a Support System for Quitting

Quitting smoking can be a challenging and overwhelming

process, but it becomes much more manageable when you have a support system in place. A support system can include friends, family, co-workers, or even professionals who can offer guidance, encouragement, and accountability during the quitting process.

One of the first steps in creating a support system is identifying the people in your life who are willing and able to help you quit smoking. These could be individuals who have already quit smoking, those who are also trying to quit, or people who are supportive of your decision to quit.

Once you have identified potential supporters, it's essential to communicate your needs and goals clearly. Let your support system know what kind of help you're looking for and how they can assist you during the quitting process. For example, you may want a friend to check in with you daily or accompany you to a support group, or you may want a family member to help you avoid triggers or provide distractions during moments of temptation.

In addition to personal support, there are also professional resources available for those looking to quit smoking. These resources can include nicotine replacement therapies, prescription medications, or counseling services. Consulting with a healthcare provider or addiction specialist can provide valuable insight and guidance on which resources may be most effective for you.

Finally, it's essential to remember that a support system is not a substitute for personal responsibility and commitment to quitting. While having a support system can make the quitting process more comfortable, it's ultimately up to the individual to make the necessary changes and remain committed to a smoke-free lifestyle.

In conclusion, creating a support system can be a vital component in successfully quitting smoking. By identifying potential supporters, communicating your needs and goals, and utilizing professional resources when necessary, you can increase your chances of long-term success and improve your overall health and well-being.

Chapter 13: Managing Stress Without Cigarettes

Stress is a common trigger for smoking, and many people who quit smoking find that they need new strategies to manage stress. Fortunately, there are many effective ways to cope with stress that don't involve smoking.

One technique is mindfulness meditation, which involves paying attention to the present moment without judgment. Studies have shown that practicing mindfulness can reduce stress and help with smoking cessation. Apps like Headspace and Calm can be helpful for beginners.

Another way to manage stress is through physical activity. Exercise releases endorphins, which can improve mood and reduce stress. Even a short walk or stretching session can be helpful.

Engaging in hobbies or activities that bring joy can also help reduce stress. Whether it's painting, reading, or playing a musical instrument, finding time to engage in enjoyable activities can provide a sense of calm and relaxation.

Finally, reaching out to a support system can be helpful in managing stress without cigarettes. Whether it's talking to a trusted friend or family member, or attending a support group, having a network of people to turn to can provide a sense of community and reduce feelings of isolation.

By practicing mindfulness, engaging in physical activity, pursuing enjoyable activities, and reaching out to others, it's possible to manage stress without cigarettes and maintain a smoke-free lifestyle.

Chapter 14: Finding New Habits to Replace Smoking

One of the hardest parts of quitting smoking is breaking the habit of reaching for a cigarette. Smoking becomes ingrained in daily routines, and it can feel like there's a void in your life once you've stopped. But finding new habits to replace smoking can help ease the transition and make quitting easier.

There are many healthy habits you can adopt to fill the gap left by smoking. For example, you could start exercising regularly, which can help improve your mood and reduce cravings. Yoga, meditation, and deep breathing exercises can also be effective for managing stress and anxiety.

In addition, you can try taking up a new hobby or pursuing an interest you've always wanted to try. This can give you a sense of purpose and help you redirect your energy and focus away from smoking. You might consider learning a new language, taking up painting, or even just reading more books.

It's important to remember that quitting smoking is a process, and it may take time to find new habits that work for you. Don't be discouraged if your first attempts at finding new habits don't feel quite right. Keep trying different things until you find what works best for you.

Finally, it's crucial to have a support system in place as you work on quitting smoking and adopting new habits. Lean on friends and family members for encouragement and seek out resources like support groups or counseling services to help you stay on track. With time, patience, and determination, you can successfully replace smoking with healthy new habits that will help you lead a smoke-free life.

Chapter 15: The Role of Exercise in Quitting Smoking

Exercise can be an effective tool for those trying to quit smoking. Not only does it provide a distraction from cravings, but it also helps to reduce stress and anxiety, which are common triggers for smoking.

Research has shown that exercise can even help to reduce nicotine cravings and withdrawal symptoms. When you exercise, your body releases endorphins, which are natural feel-good chemicals that can help to counteract the negative feelings associated with nicotine withdrawal.

Incorporating regular exercise into your quitting plan can also help you to stay motivated and focused on your goals. Whether you choose to go for a run, take a yoga class, or join a gym, finding an activity that you enjoy can make it easier to stick to your new smoke-free lifestyle.

It's important to start slowly and gradually increase the intensity and duration of your workouts over time. This will help you to avoid injury and burnout, and will also ensure that you're able to maintain a consistent exercise routine.

Remember, quitting smoking is a journey, and incorporating exercise into your plan can be a valuable tool in helping you to achieve your goals. So get moving and enjoy the many benefits of a smoke-free, healthy lifestyle!

Chapter 16: Using Nicotine Replacement Therapy

Nicotine replacement therapy (NRT) is a type of treatment that helps reduce withdrawal symptoms and cravings associated with quitting smoking. In this chapter, we'll explore the different forms of NRT, including nicotine gum, patches, lozenges, inhalers, and nasal sprays, and how they can be used to support smoking cessation.

NRT works by providing the body with small amounts of nicotine to help reduce cravings and withdrawal symptoms. This helps smokers gradually wean themselves off nicotine and reduce their dependence on cigarettes. One of the benefits of NRT is that it can be used in conjunction with other smoking cessation methods, such as counseling or support groups, to increase the chances of success.

Nicotine gum, lozenges, inhalers, and nasal sprays are all available over-the-counter, while nicotine patches require a prescription. Each type of NRT works differently and may be better suited to different individuals, depending on their preferences and smoking habits.

It's important to note that NRT is not a magic bullet and may not work for everyone. It's also essential to follow the instructions for use carefully and seek advice from a healthcare provider or addiction specialist before starting NRT. Overuse of NRT can lead to side effects such as nausea, headaches, and dizziness.

In summary, NRT can be an effective tool for smokers who want to quit smoking cigarettes. When used as directed, it can help reduce cravings and withdrawal symptoms, making it easier to quit smoking for good. However, it's important to use NRT as part of a comprehensive smoking cessation plan that includes counseling, support, and lifestyle changes.

Chapter 17: Medications to Help You Quit Smoking

While quitting smoking can be challenging, there are medications available that can help you overcome nicotine addiction and manage withdrawal symptoms. Here are some of the medications that can help you quit smoking:

Nicotine Replacement Therapy (NRT): NRT comes in many forms, including gum, patches, lozenges, inhalers, and nasal sprays. These products deliver nicotine to your body without the harmful chemicals found in cigarettes, and can help alleviate withdrawal symptoms like cravings, irritability, and restlessness.

Bupropion (Zyban): Bupropion is an antidepressant that can also help you quit smoking. It works by reducing nicotine cravings and withdrawal symptoms and is taken in pill form.

Varenicline (Chantix): Varenicline is a medication that blocks nicotine receptors in the brain, reducing the pleasurable effects of smoking. It also helps to alleviate withdrawal symptoms and cravings, and is taken in pill form.

It's important to note that these medications work best when used as part of a comprehensive smoking cessation program, which may include counseling, support groups, and lifestyle changes. Talk to your healthcare provider about which medication may be right for you, and always follow the recommended dosages and instructions for use.

Chapter 18: Quitting Smoking and Weight Gain

One of the biggest concerns for smokers who want to quit is the potential for weight gain. Many people who quit smoking find that they gain weight, which can be discouraging and make it more difficult to stay smoke-free. However, weight gain should not deter you from quitting smoking.

Nicotine is known to suppress appetite and increase metabolism, which is why smokers often find it easier to maintain a healthy weight. When you quit smoking, your metabolism slows down, and your appetite may increase, leading to weight gain. However, weight gain is a small price to pay for the many benefits of quitting smoking.

It's important to remember that weight gain after quitting smoking is not inevitable. There are steps you can take to minimize weight gain while quitting, such as incorporating regular physical activity into your routine and making healthier food choices. Staying active can help boost your metabolism and burn calories, while healthy food choices can keep you feeling full and satisfied without packing on the pounds.

In addition, it's essential to have realistic expectations about your weight and body image after quitting smoking. Weight gain is a natural part of the process, and it may take some time to reach your ideal weight. Focus on the positive changes you're making for your health, and don't get too caught up in the number on the scale.

If you do experience weight gain after quitting smoking, remember that it's a temporary side effect that can be managed with healthy habits. Don't let the fear of weight gain hold you back from quitting smoking and improving your health in many other ways. With the right mindset and strategies, you can quit smoking and maintain a healthy weight at the same time.

Chapter 19: Managing Your Diet During Quitting

When you quit smoking, your body undergoes various changes that can affect your appetite and eating habits. Some people may experience increased cravings for sugar or junk food, while others may lose their appetite altogether. It's important to manage your diet during this time to ensure that you're providing your body with the proper nutrients it needs to function properly.

First, it's essential to stay hydrated. Drinking plenty of water can help flush toxins out of your system and curb cravings. You may also want to consider adding some herbal teas or other low-sugar beverages to your diet to help replace the act of smoking.

Next, focus on eating a balanced diet that includes plenty of fruits, vegetables, lean protein, and whole grains. These foods can provide your body with essential vitamins and nutrients to help keep your immune system functioning properly, boost your energy levels, and reduce cravings.

It's also important to avoid triggers that may make you want to smoke, such as drinking alcohol or consuming too much caffeine. Instead, try to incorporate healthy snacks into your routine, such as nuts, seeds, and fresh fruit, to help curb cravings and keep you feeling full.

Finally, be patient with yourself. It's common to experience changes in appetite and cravings during the quitting process, but with time and dedication, you can manage your diet and maintain a healthy lifestyle. Remember to listen to your body, stay active, and seek support from loved ones or healthcare professionals if needed.

Chapter 20: Avoiding Alcohol and Other Triggers

Alcohol and other triggers can be powerful influences on smoking behavior. Many smokers report that they are more likely to smoke when they are drinking alcohol, for example. In order to successfully quit smoking, it's important to identify and avoid triggers that can lead to smoking.

One of the most effective ways to avoid triggers is to change your routine. If you typically smoke while drinking coffee in the morning, for example, try drinking tea instead. Or if you tend to smoke when you're stressed, try taking a walk or practicing deep breathing exercises instead.

Avoiding alcohol can also be helpful in quitting smoking. Alcohol can lower inhibitions and make it more difficult to resist smoking. If you find it difficult to avoid alcohol altogether, try limiting your intake or avoiding situations where you know you'll be tempted to smoke.

Other common triggers for smoking include social situations, stress, and certain emotions. To avoid these triggers, consider changing your social activities or seeking support from friends and family. Practicing stress-reducing techniques, such as yoga or meditation, can also be helpful.

Remember, quitting smoking is a process, and it's normal to experience cravings and setbacks. By identifying and avoiding triggers, you can make the process easier and increase your chances of success. Stay committed to your goal and seek support when you need it.

Chapter 21: Dealing with Relapse

Quitting smoking is a challenging journey, and it's not uncommon for people to experience relapse. If you slip up and smoke a cigarette, it doesn't mean that you've failed or that you can't quit for good. It's essential to learn how to deal with relapse and get back on track.

The first step in dealing with relapse is to acknowledge it. Recognize that you smoked a cigarette and that you slipped up. Don't beat yourself up or feel guilty about it; instead, use it as an opportunity to learn and grow.

The next step is to identify the trigger that caused you to smoke. Was it stress, boredom, or peer pressure? Once you've identified the trigger, come up with a plan to avoid it in the future. For example, if stress is a trigger, you can practice relaxation techniques or engage in physical activity to reduce stress.

It's also helpful to remind yourself of the reasons why you quit smoking in the first place. Write down your motivations and keep them handy, so you can refer to them when you feel tempted to smoke again. Remember that quitting smoking is a process, and it's normal to experience setbacks.

Seeking support is also crucial when dealing with relapse. Talk to friends and family members who understand your journey and can offer encouragement and motivation. You can also seek support from healthcare professionals or addiction specialists who can help you develop coping strategies and address any underlying issues that may have contributed to your relapse.

In conclusion, dealing with relapse is an important part of quitting smoking. It's essential to acknowledge it, identify the trigger, come up with a plan to avoid it, remind yourself of your motivations, and seek support. With persistence and determination, you can overcome relapse and achieve a smoke-free lifestyle.

Chapter 22: Revisiting Your Reasons for Quitting Smoking

When you first decided to quit smoking, you likely had a set of reasons in mind. Maybe you wanted to improve your health, save money, or set a positive example for your loved ones. Whatever your reasons, it's important to revisit them regularly throughout your quitting journey.

One reason to revisit your reasons for quitting is that they can help you stay motivated. When you're feeling tempted to smoke, reminding yourself of why you wanted to quit in the first place can help you stay strong and resist the urge. Your reasons can also serve as a source of inspiration, reminding you of the positive changes you've already made and the progress you've achieved.

Another reason to revisit your reasons for quitting is that they can evolve over time. As you continue on your quitting journey, you may find that your motivations change or become more refined. For example, you may have initially quit smoking to improve your overall health, but as time goes on, you may also start to appreciate the benefits of having a cleaner, fresher-smelling home or car.

To revisit your reasons for quitting, start by taking a few minutes to reflect on what motivated you to quit in the first place. Write down your reasons, whether in a journal, on a notepad, or in a digital document. Then, take some time to assess how your reasons have evolved or changed over time. Are there new motivations that have emerged? Have any of your original reasons become less important to you?

Finally, use your reasons for quitting as a source of strength and inspiration throughout your journey. When you're feeling tempted to smoke, take a moment to review your list and remind yourself of why you're making this important change. By keeping your reasons for quitting at the forefront of your mind, you can stay motivated, focused, and committed to a smoke-free life.

Chapter 23: The Benefits of Quitting Smoking for Your Loved Ones

Quitting smoking is not only beneficial for your own health, but it can also have a positive impact on your loved ones. Smoking is a major risk factor for numerous health problems, and it can even lead to premature death. By quitting smoking, you can reduce the risk of developing smoking-related health issues and extend your life expectancy. But the benefits of quitting smoking extend beyond your own personal health.

One of the biggest benefits of quitting smoking is that you can protect your loved ones from the dangers of secondhand smoke. Secondhand smoke is a mixture of the smoke exhaled by the smoker and the smoke from the burning cigarette, and it can be just as harmful as smoking itself. Secondhand smoke exposure can increase the risk of heart disease, lung cancer, and other health problems in non-smokers, particularly children and infants.

When you quit smoking, you not only reduce your own exposure to harmful chemicals, but you also reduce the amount of secondhand smoke that your loved ones are exposed to. This can have a significant positive impact on their health and wellbeing. Additionally, quitting smoking can also set a positive example for your children and loved ones, and encourage them to lead healthier lifestyles.

In addition to protecting your loved ones from secondhand smoke, quitting smoking can also improve your relationships with them. Smoking can create tension and conflict in relationships, particularly if your loved ones are concerned about your health or find the smell of smoke unpleasant. By quitting smoking, you can show your loved ones that you care about your health and their wellbeing, and strengthen your relationships with them.

In conclusion, quitting smoking can have numerous benefits for your loved ones, including reducing their exposure to secondhand smoke, improving your relationships with them, and setting a positive example for healthy living. So, when you're struggling with quitting, remember that you're not only doing it for yourself but also for the people you care about.

Chapter 24: Preparing for Social Situations Without Smoking

One of the biggest challenges of quitting smoking is learning how to navigate social situations without lighting up. Whether it's a party, a night out with friends, or a family gathering, social situations can be a trigger for cravings and make it difficult to stick to your goal of being smoke-free. Here are some tips for preparing for social situations without smoking:

Have a Plan: Before you go to a social event, make a plan for how you will deal with cravings or triggers. Think about what activities you can do to distract yourself, such as playing a game, dancing, or socializing with non-smokers.

Bring Support: Having a support system can make a big difference in staying smoke-free in social situations. Consider bringing a friend who is also trying to quit smoking or who can help keep you accountable.

Avoid Triggers: Identify the triggers that may make you want to smoke, such as being around other smokers or drinking alcohol. If possible, avoid these triggers or limit your exposure to them.

Practice Saying No: Be prepared to say no if someone offers you a cigarette. It can be helpful to practice saying no in advance so you feel more confident when the situation arises.

Use Nicotine Replacement Therapy: Consider using nicotine replacement therapy, such as gum or patches, to help reduce cravings during social situations.

Remember, quitting smoking is a journey, and it's okay to slip up from time to time. What's important is that you stay committed to your goal and continue to learn new ways to stay smoke-free in different situations. With practice and persistence, you can overcome the challenge of social situations without smoking and enjoy a healthier, smoke-free life.

Chapter 25: Understanding the Psychological Addiction to Smoking

Nicotine is known to be a highly addictive substance that creates a physical dependence on smoking. However, many smokers find that the psychological addiction to smoking can be just as difficult to overcome.

Psychological addiction to smoking is characterized by a strong emotional and mental attachment to smoking. Smokers may associate smoking with certain activities or emotions, such as relaxation, socializing, or stress relief. These associations can become so ingrained that smokers feel like they cannot perform these activities or manage these emotions without smoking.

Many smokers also experience a sense of loss or anxiety when they consider quitting smoking. Smoking may have become an important part of their identity or daily routine, and the idea of giving it up can be overwhelming.

It is important to understand the psychological addiction to smoking in order to successfully quit. Quitting smoking may require breaking down these emotional and mental associations with smoking, and finding new ways to manage stress or engage in activities that were previously associated with smoking.

One effective way to address the psychological addiction to smoking is through behavioral therapy. Behavioral therapy can help smokers identify their emotional triggers for smoking and develop new coping mechanisms to address these triggers.

Ultimately, it is important for smokers to understand that quitting smoking is not just about breaking a physical addiction, but also a psychological one. By recognizing and addressing the psychological addiction to smoking, smokers can increase their chances of successfully quitting and maintaining a smoke-free lifestyle.

Chapter 26: The Power of Positive Thinking in Quitting Smoking

Quitting smoking can be a challenging journey, but it can also be an opportunity for personal growth and self-discovery. The way we think about ourselves and our ability to quit smoking can have a significant impact on our success. The power of positive thinking can help us overcome obstacles, stay motivated, and ultimately quit smoking for good.

Negative thoughts and self-doubt can be major barriers to quitting smoking. Thoughts like "I can't do it" or "I'll never be able to quit" can make the process seem overwhelming and impossible. But with a positive mindset, we can reframe these thoughts and approach quitting with confidence and determination.

One way to cultivate a positive mindset is through daily affirmations. Affirmations are positive statements that we repeat to ourselves to reinforce our beliefs and values. Some examples of affirmations for quitting smoking include "I am a non-smoker," "I am strong and capable," and "I am in control of my choices." By repeating these affirmations daily, we can shift our mindset and focus on our strengths and abilities rather than our perceived limitations.

Another way to harness the power of positive thinking is through visualization. Visualization involves creating a mental image of ourselves as non-smokers and visualizing ourselves succeeding in our quit journey. We can also visualize the benefits of quitting smoking, such as improved health, increased energy, and greater financial stability. Visualization can help us stay motivated and focused on our goals.

Finally, it's important to surround ourselves with positive influences and support systems. Whether it's through online support groups, counseling, or connecting with friends and family who have quit smoking, having a supportive community can make a significant difference in our quit journey. By focusing on positive influences and support, we can stay motivated and continue to cultivate a positive mindset.

In conclusion, the power of positive thinking can be a valuable tool in quitting smoking. By cultivating a positive mindset through daily affirmations, visualization, and surrounding ourselves with positive influences, we can overcome obstacles and stay motivated on our quit journey. Remember, quitting smoking is not just about breaking a habit; it's also about cultivating a healthier and happier life.

Chapter 27: Keeping a Quit Smoking Journal

Keeping a journal can be a helpful tool in your journey to quit smoking. By tracking your progress, reflecting on your thoughts and feelings, and identifying triggers and patterns, you can gain a deeper understanding of your relationship with smoking and increase your chances of success.

To start, choose a notebook or journal that you enjoy writing in. Set aside a few minutes each day to record your thoughts and experiences related to quitting smoking. You might want to include the following information:

The date and time of each cigarette you smoke.

The circumstances surrounding each cigarette, such as where you were, who you were with, and what you were doing.

Your cravings and how you dealt with them.

Your thoughts and feelings about quitting smoking.

Any challenges or obstacles you faced, and how you overcame them.

The positive changes you notice as you reduce or eliminate smoking from your life.

As you write in your journal, try to be honest and non-judgmental with yourself. Remember that quitting smoking is a process, and it's normal to experience setbacks or difficult emotions along the way. Use your journal as a tool for self-reflection and growth, rather than as a way to beat yourself up for mistakes or slip-ups.

Reviewing your journal periodically can be a powerful way to see how far you've come and identify areas where you may need additional support. It can also serve as a source of inspiration and motivation, reminding you of your goals and the progress you've made. Consider sharing your journal with a trusted friend, family member, or healthcare provider who can offer encouragement and support as you continue on your journey to a smoke-free life.

Chapter 28: The Importance of Sleep During Quitting

Quitting smoking can have a profound impact on your body, both physically and mentally. One of the biggest challenges you may face during the quitting process is sleep disruption. Nicotine withdrawal can cause insomnia and other sleep disturbances, making it difficult to get the rest you need. However, getting enough sleep is crucial for your overall health and can make the quitting process easier. In this chapter, we'll explore the importance of sleep during quitting and provide tips for improving sleep hygiene.

Lack of sleep can lead to irritability, poor concentration, and a weakened immune system, making it harder to cope with nicotine withdrawal and other challenges that come with quitting smoking. In addition, sleep deprivation can increase cravings for nicotine, leading to a higher risk of relapse. Therefore, it's essential to prioritize sleep during the quitting process.

There are several steps you can take to improve your sleep hygiene while quitting smoking. Firstly, it's important to establish a regular sleep schedule and stick to it as much as possible. This can help regulate your body's natural sleep-wake cycle and promote better quality sleep. Secondly, avoid nicotine and caffeine before bedtime, as they can interfere with sleep. Instead, opt for relaxation techniques like deep breathing or meditation to calm your mind and prepare for sleep.

It's also important to create a sleep-conducive environment. Make sure your bedroom is quiet, dark, and cool, and remove any distractions that may interfere with sleep, such as electronic devices or a television. Finally, if you're still struggling with sleep disruption, consider talking to your healthcare provider about other strategies that may help, such as cognitive behavioral therapy for insomnia or medication.

In conclusion, getting enough sleep is crucial for your overall health and can make the quitting process easier. By prioritizing sleep hygiene and seeking professional support if needed, you can improve your chances of successfully quitting smoking and maintaining a smoke-free lifestyle.

Chapter 29: Quitting Smoking and Your Finances

Smoking is not only harmful to your health, but it can also

take a significant toll on your finances. Cigarettes are expensive, and the costs can add up quickly, especially if you smoke a pack a day or more. When you quit smoking, you can save a considerable amount of money over time.

Let's take a closer look at how quitting smoking can impact your finances:

Saving Money on Cigarettes: The most obvious way quitting smoking can impact your finances is by saving money on cigarettes. Depending on where you live, a pack of cigarettes can cost anywhere from a few dollars to over ten dollars. If you smoke a pack a day, that's hundreds of dollars a month you could be saving by quitting.

Avoiding Health-Related Expenses: Smoking can also lead to a range of health problems, including lung cancer, heart disease, and respiratory issues. These health problems can result in expensive medical bills, medications, and hospitalizations. By quitting smoking, you can reduce your risk of these health problems and avoid the associated expenses.

Improving Your Job Prospects: Smoking can also impact your job prospects. Many employers now have policies against smoking, and some may even require employees to pass a nicotine test before being hired. By quitting smoking, you can open up new job opportunities and potentially earn more money.

Lowering Insurance Premiums: Finally, quitting smoking can also lead to lower insurance premiums. Health and life insurance companies often charge smokers higher premiums due to the increased health risks associated with smoking. By quitting smoking, you can potentially save money on your insurance premiums.

In conclusion, quitting smoking can have a positive impact on your finances in several ways. By saving money on cigarettes, avoiding health-related expenses, improving your job prospects, and potentially lowering your insurance premiums, you can improve your financial well-being and enjoy the benefits of a smoke-free life.

Chapter 30: Dealing with Work Stress Without Smoking

Stress at work can be a major trigger for smokers trying to quit, but it's important to find alternative coping mechanisms to avoid relapse. Here are some strategies for dealing with work stress without smoking:

Take breaks: When you feel stressed, take a short break from work to clear your mind. Go for a walk, stretch, or practice some deep breathing exercises.

Practice mindfulness: Mindfulness techniques such as meditation or yoga can help reduce stress and promote relaxation. Try incorporating a short mindfulness practice into your daily routine, whether it's during your lunch break or before you start your workday.

Prioritize self-care: Make time for activities that help you relax and recharge outside of work, such as exercise, hobbies, or spending time with loved ones.

Communicate with your boss: If work stress is becoming overwhelming, consider speaking with your boss or HR representative about ways to reduce your workload or improve your work environment.

Seek support: If you're struggling with work stress or the quitting process in general, seek support from friends, family, or a support group. Remember that quitting smoking is a journey, and it's okay to ask for help along the way.

Chapter 31: Finding New Hobbies to Replace Smoking

Smoking can become a habit that occupies a significant amount of time in a smoker's life. Quitting smoking not only frees up that time but also leaves a void that can be difficult to fill. One way to overcome this challenge is to find new hobbies to replace smoking. Here are some ideas to get started:

Exercise: Physical activity is a great way to boost mood, relieve stress, and distract from cravings. Consider taking up jogging, yoga, cycling, or joining a fitness class.

Artistic Pursuits: Creating art can be a therapeutic and meditative activity that can be a good substitute for smoking. Consider trying painting, drawing, photography, or pottery.

Music: Learning to play an instrument or listening to music can be a good way to distract from cravings and fill the void left by smoking.

Reading: Reading can be an excellent way to relax and distract from cravings. Consider joining a book club or finding a new book series to read.

Volunteering: Volunteering can provide a sense of purpose and fulfillment. Consider volunteering at a local charity or community organization.

Cooking: Cooking can be a healthy and productive way to occupy time and explore new flavors. Consider trying new recipes or taking a cooking class.

Outdoor Activities: Spending time in nature can be a good way to reduce stress and improve mood. Consider hiking, camping, fishing, or gardening.

By finding new hobbies to replace smoking, smokers can restructure their lives and reduce the likelihood of relapse. It is essential to remember that finding new hobbies takes time, and it's okay to try different activities before finding the ones that work best. The most important thing is to remain committed to quitting smoking and exploring new ways to live a healthy, smoke-free life.

Chapter 32: Quitting Smoking and Your Appearance

Smoking not only affects your health, but it can also have a significant impact on your appearance. Many smokers develop a yellow or gray tint to their skin and teeth, and smoking can also lead to premature wrinkles, fine lines, and other skin damage.

When you quit smoking, you may notice some positive changes in your appearance. Within just a few days of quitting, your skin may start to look brighter and healthier as it begins to repair itself. Over time, your skin may become clearer and more even-toned, and you may notice a reduction in fine lines and wrinkles.

Quitting smoking can also have a positive impact on your dental health. Smoking can cause tooth staining and discoloration, as well as contribute to gum disease and tooth loss. When you quit smoking, you may notice that your teeth begin to look whiter and brighter, and your gums may become healthier.

Another benefit of quitting smoking is the reduction in the smell of cigarette smoke on your clothes, hair, and breath. This can lead to a fresher, more pleasant smell overall, and can also help to improve your confidence and self-esteem.

If you're concerned about the impact of smoking on your appearance, quitting smoking can be a positive step towards improving your overall health and well-being, as well as your physical appearance. Remember, the benefits of quitting smoking extend far beyond just your appearance, and can also improve your lung function, reduce your risk of disease, and increase your lifespan.

Chapter 33: The Role of Family and Friends in Quitting Smoking

Quitting smoking can be challenging, but having a support system can make all the difference. The support of family and friends can provide encouragement, motivation, and accountability during the quitting process.

Involving loved ones in your quit plan can also help to reduce stress and provide a sense of community. Letting family and friends know that you are quitting can create a positive atmosphere of support and understanding.

Your family and friends can also play a practical role in helping you quit smoking. They can help you identify triggers, provide distractions during cravings, and even join you in adopting a healthier lifestyle.

However, it's important to be mindful of how you approach your loved ones for support. Some people may not be familiar with addiction or may not understand the challenges of quitting smoking. It's essential to communicate your needs and be open to feedback and suggestions.

In summary, involving family and friends in your quit plan can provide essential support and encouragement during the quitting process. Don't be afraid to reach out and ask for help, and remember to communicate your needs and be receptive to feedback. Together, you can create a supportive environment that promotes a healthy, smoke-free lifestyle.

Chapter 34: Celebrating Your Milestones in Quitting

Quitting smoking is not an easy journey, but it is an incredibly rewarding one. Every milestone you reach, no matter how small, is a cause for celebration. By recognizing and celebrating your achievements, you can stay motivated and committed to your goal of living a smoke-free life.

One way to celebrate your milestones is by setting goals and rewarding yourself when you achieve them. For example, you might set a goal to go one week without smoking, and then treat yourself to a special dinner or a new piece of clothing when you reach that goal. As you progress, you can set larger goals and more significant rewards.

Another way to celebrate your milestones is by sharing your success with others. Tell your friends and family about your progress and ask them to join you in celebrating your achievements. You might even inspire others to quit smoking themselves.

It's important to remember that celebrating your milestones doesn't have to involve spending a lot of money or doing something extravagant. Simple gestures like treating yourself to your favorite snack, taking a relaxing bath, or enjoying a nature walk can be just as rewarding.

However, it's important to avoid celebrating with things that could potentially lead to relapse, such as alcohol or other drugs. Instead, focus on celebrating in healthy and positive ways.

In summary, celebrating your milestones is a crucial part of quitting smoking. It can help you stay motivated, committed, and proud of your accomplishments. So take the time to recognize your achievements, no matter how small, and celebrate in ways that are positive, healthy, and inspiring.

Chapter 35: The Health Benefits of Quitting Smoking Long-Term

Quitting smoking is one of the best things you can do for your health. While the immediate benefits of quitting smoking, such as improved breathing and a sense of accomplishment, are well known, the long-term health benefits are even more significant. In this chapter, we'll explore the health benefits of quitting smoking in the long term and how they can improve your overall quality of life.

First and foremost, quitting smoking greatly reduces your risk of developing serious health conditions, including lung cancer, heart disease, stroke, and respiratory diseases like chronic bronchitis and emphysema. According to the Centers for Disease Control and Prevention (CDC), people who quit smoking reduce their risk of these conditions over time, and after 10 to 15 years of not smoking, their risk of these diseases is similar to that of someone who never smoked.

Quitting smoking can also improve your overall physical health. Smoking damages your lungs, reduces your lung capacity, and makes it harder to breathe. When you quit smoking, your lung function begins to improve immediately, and over time, your risk of lung diseases decreases significantly. Additionally, quitting smoking can help reduce inflammation in your body, which can lead to a host of other health benefits, such as better digestion, clearer skin, and improved immune function.

Perhaps one of the most significant long-term health benefits of quitting smoking is the increased lifespan it can provide. According to the American Cancer Society, quitting smoking before the age of 40 can add up to 10 years to your life expectancy. Even quitting after the age of 40 can still provide significant health benefits and increase your chances of living a longer, healthier life.

In summary, quitting smoking provides a wide range of long-term health benefits that can greatly improve your quality of life. From reducing your risk of serious health conditions to improving your lung function and increasing your lifespan, quitting smoking is one of the best things you can do for your overall health and wellbeing.

Chapter 36: The Risks of Secondhand Smoke

Smoking doesn't just affect the smoker - it also affects those around them. Secondhand smoke, the smoke that's exhaled by a smoker or comes from the burning end of a cigarette, can be just as dangerous as smoking itself.

The dangers of secondhand smoke are numerous. Exposure to secondhand smoke has been linked to an increased risk of lung cancer, heart disease, stroke, and respiratory illnesses such as asthma and bronchitis. Children are particularly vulnerable to the effects of secondhand smoke, as their lungs are still developing and they breathe more rapidly than adults. Secondhand smoke exposure in children has been linked to sudden infant death syndrome (SIDS), low birth weight, and a higher risk of developing asthma and other respiratory illnesses.

Even brief exposure to secondhand smoke can be harmful. The toxins in cigarette smoke can linger in the air for hours after smoking has stopped, putting those in the immediate vicinity at risk. The only way to fully protect oneself and others from the dangers of secondhand smoke is to quit smoking entirely.

Quitting smoking not only benefits the smoker's health but also the health of those around them. By quitting, smokers can protect their loved ones from the harmful effects of secondhand smoke and create a healthier environment for everyone. If you're struggling to quit smoking, keep in mind that your efforts are not just for yourself - they're for those you care about as well.

Chapter 37: The Benefits of Clean Air in Your Home

When you're trying to quit smoking, it's important to

create a supportive environment that encourages healthy behaviors. One way to do this is by ensuring that the air in your home is clean and free of pollutants.

Clean air has numerous benefits for your health, including:

Improved Respiratory Health: When you breathe in clean air, your lungs can function more efficiently, allowing you to breathe more easily. This is particularly important if you suffer from respiratory conditions such as asthma or chronic obstructive pulmonary disease (COPD).

Reduced Risk of Infection: Clean air can help reduce the spread of viruses and bacteria, reducing your risk of developing infections such as the flu or COVID-19.

Increased Energy: When you breathe in clean air, your body can more effectively deliver oxygen to your cells, boosting your energy levels and reducing fatigue.

Better Sleep: Poor air quality can disrupt your sleep, leading to a host of negative health outcomes. Clean air can help improve the quality of your sleep, allowing you to wake up feeling more rested and refreshed.

To improve the air quality in your home, there are several steps you can take. These include:

Invest in an air purifier: An air purifier can help remove pollutants and allergens from the air, creating a cleaner and healthier environment.

Use natural cleaning products: Many household cleaning products contain harsh chemicals that can negatively impact air quality. Switching to natural cleaning products can help reduce the amount of toxins in your home.

Open windows and doors: Allowing fresh air to circulate through your home can help reduce the concentration of pollutants and improve air quality.

By taking steps to improve the air quality in your home, you can create a healthier and more supportive environment for your journey to quit smoking.

Chapter 38: The Effects of Smoking on Your Oral Health

Smoking is not only harmful to your lungs and heart but can also have a severe impact on your oral health. Tobacco products contain harmful chemicals that can damage your teeth, gums, and mouth. Here are some of the ways that smoking can affect your oral health:

Bad breath: Smoking is a significant cause of bad breath. The chemicals in cigarettes can leave a lingering smell in your mouth, making your breath smell unpleasant.

Yellowed teeth: Smoking can cause your teeth to become stained and yellowed over time. The nicotine and tar in tobacco products can seep into the pores of your teeth, leaving behind a stubborn stain that can be challenging to remove.

Gum disease: Smoking weakens your immune system and damages the tissues in your mouth, making you more susceptible to gum disease. This condition can cause swollen, bleeding gums and tooth loss.

Oral cancer: Smoking is a significant risk factor for oral cancer. The harmful chemicals in tobacco products can damage the cells in your mouth and throat, leading to cancerous growths.

Delayed healing: Smokers often experience delayed healing after dental procedures, such as tooth extractions or gum surgery. This is because smoking impairs blood flow, making it harder for your body to heal itself.

Quitting smoking can have a significant impact on your oral health. Within a few weeks of quitting, you may notice improvements in your breath, teeth, and gums. Over time, your risk of developing gum disease and oral cancer may also decrease. If you're struggling to quit smoking, talk to your dentist or healthcare provider about resources that can help you kick the habit for good.

Chapter 39: The Benefits of Clearing Your Lungs After Quitting

After quitting smoking, your lungs begin the process of healing and clearing out the harmful substances left behind by cigarettes. While it may take some time to notice significant improvements, clearing your lungs can have several benefits for your health and overall well-being.

Firstly, clearing your lungs can help improve your breathing. Smoking can damage your lungs and make it more difficult to breathe, but as you clear out the harmful substances left behind by cigarettes, you may notice that you breathe more easily and have more stamina during physical activity.

Additionally, clearing your lungs can help reduce your risk of lung cancer and other respiratory illnesses. Smoking is a leading cause of lung cancer, but quitting smoking and clearing your lungs can help lower your risk of developing this and other respiratory diseases.

Furthermore, clearing your lungs can also lead to improved sense of taste and smell. Smoking can affect your taste buds and olfactory receptors, making it difficult to fully enjoy food and appreciate aromas. However, as you clear out the harmful substances left behind by cigarettes, you may notice an improvement in your ability to taste and smell.

Finally, clearing your lungs can help you feel more energetic and improve your overall sense of well-being. Smoking can cause fatigue and drain your energy levels, but as your lungs clear, you may feel more alert, focused, and ready to tackle the day.

In conclusion, clearing your lungs after quitting smoking can have numerous benefits for your health and overall well-being. It may take some time, but with patience and perseverance, you can achieve a healthier, smoke-free lifestyle.

Chapter 40: The Effects of Smoking on Your Skin

While most people are aware of the health risks associated with smoking, fewer may be aware of the impact it has on their skin. Smoking can cause a wide range of negative effects on the skin, including premature aging, skin discoloration, and a higher risk of skin cancer.

One of the most noticeable effects of smoking on the skin is premature aging. Smoking can cause the skin to lose elasticity and firmness, resulting in wrinkles and fine lines appearing earlier than they would in non-smokers. This is because smoking damages the collagen and elastin fibers that keep the skin looking youthful.

Smoking can also cause skin discoloration. Nicotine and other chemicals in tobacco smoke can restrict blood flow to the skin, resulting in a yellow or grayish tint to the skin. Smokers may also experience uneven skin tone and dark circles under the eyes, which can be difficult to conceal with makeup.

Furthermore, smoking increases the risk of developing certain types of skin cancer. Studies have found that smokers are more likely to develop squamous cell carcinoma, a type of skin cancer that can be aggressive and spread quickly. Smoking may also increase the risk of developing melanoma, the deadliest form of skin cancer.

Quitting smoking can have a positive impact on the skin, improving its appearance and reducing the risk of skin cancer. Within a few weeks of quitting smoking, blood flow to the skin begins to improve, resulting in a brighter, more even complexion. Over time, wrinkles and fine lines may also begin to fade.

In conclusion, smoking has a detrimental impact on the skin, causing premature aging, skin discoloration, and an increased risk of skin cancer. Quitting smoking can help to reverse some of these effects and improve the overall health and appearance of your skin.

Chapter 41: The Role of Mindfulness in Quitting Smoking

Mindfulness is a practice that involves being present in the moment, without judgment or distraction. It can be an effective tool for those trying to quit smoking, as it can help reduce stress and anxiety, two common triggers for smoking. In this chapter, we'll explore the role of mindfulness in quitting smoking and how it can help you achieve your goals.

Firstly, mindfulness can help you become more aware of your thoughts and feelings. This self-awareness can help you identify the triggers that lead to smoking and give you the power to respond to those triggers in a healthy way. By being mindful, you can learn to recognize the urge to smoke and acknowledge it without giving in to it.

Secondly, mindfulness can help you manage stress and anxiety. Quitting smoking can be a stressful and anxiety-inducing experience, but mindfulness practices like meditation and deep breathing can help calm the mind and body. These practices can also help you develop resilience and cope with the challenges of quitting smoking.

Finally, mindfulness can help you stay focused and motivated during the quitting process. By staying present in the moment, you can avoid getting caught up in worries about the future or regrets about the past. Instead, you can focus on the benefits of quitting smoking and the progress you've made so far.

Incorporating mindfulness practices into your daily routine can be a powerful tool for quitting smoking. Consider adding mindfulness practices like meditation, deep breathing, or yoga to your daily routine. You may also find it helpful to seek out a mindfulness coach or attend a mindfulness-based smoking cessation program.

Remember, mindfulness is a practice, and it takes time and patience to develop. Be kind to yourself as you begin your mindfulness journey and keep in mind that it can take time to see the benefits. But with persistence and dedication, you can develop a mindfulness practice that helps you quit smoking for good.

Chapter 42: Dealing with Cravings and Negative Emotions

One of the most challenging aspects of quitting smoking is dealing with cravings and negative emotions that may arise during the process. Cravings are a natural part of nicotine withdrawal, and they can be triggered by a variety of factors, including stress, anxiety, and boredom.

Here are some tips for dealing with cravings and negative emotions during the quitting process:

Practice Mindfulness: When a craving or negative emotion arises, take a moment to pause and observe the sensation without judgment. Mindfulness can help you become more aware of your thoughts and feelings, allowing you to respond to them in a more constructive way.

Engage in a Relaxation Technique: Practicing relaxation techniques such as deep breathing, yoga, or meditation can help reduce stress and anxiety, which can trigger cravings. Find a technique that works for you and practice it regularly.

Distract Yourself: When a craving hits, try to distract yourself with a healthy activity, such as exercise, reading, or spending time with friends and family. Finding something else to focus on can help reduce the intensity of the craving.

Reach Out for Support: Don't be afraid to reach out to friends, family, or a support group for help when you're struggling with cravings or negative emotions. Talking to someone who understands what you're going through can help you feel less alone and more motivated to stay on track.

Remember Your Motivation: Whenever you're feeling tempted to smoke, remind yourself of why you decided to quit in the first place. Keep a list of your reasons for quitting handy, and review it whenever you need a reminder of the benefits of a smoke-free life.

Dealing with cravings and negative emotions can be difficult, but it's important to remember that they are temporary and will pass. With the right mindset and support, you can overcome them and continue on your journey towards a healthier, smoke-free life.

Chapter 43: The Importance of Oral Health After Quitting

Quitting smoking can do wonders for your overall health, and it can also greatly improve the health of your mouth. Smoking has a significant impact on oral health, and quitting can help reverse some of the damage caused by years of smoking.

One of the most noticeable improvements after quitting smoking is the reduction in yellowing of teeth and the removal of tobacco stains. Smoking also contributes to gum disease and bad breath. When you quit smoking, your gums will become healthier, and your breath will be fresher.

The long-term effects of smoking can lead to more severe dental issues, such as gum disease and tooth loss. Smoking also decreases the amount of oxygen in your bloodstream, which can make it harder for your gums to heal.

After quitting smoking, it is important to maintain good oral hygiene to prevent any further damage to your mouth. Brushing twice a day, flossing daily, and regular dental check-ups can help keep your mouth healthy and reduce the risk of dental problems.

In addition to maintaining good oral hygiene, it is also essential to stay hydrated and avoid sugary or acidic drinks and foods that can damage your teeth. Drinking water and consuming healthy snacks, such as fruits and vegetables, can also help improve your oral health.

Overall, quitting smoking can have a positive impact on your oral health, but it is important to be proactive about maintaining good oral hygiene to prevent any further damage.

Chapter 44: Using Positive Affirmations in Quitting Smoking

Positive affirmations are statements that can help you shift your mindset and focus on positive thinking. When it comes to quitting smoking, affirmations can be a powerful tool to help you stay motivated and committed to your goal. Here are some tips for using positive affirmations in your journey to quit smoking:

Identify Your Affirmations: Take some time to identify the affirmations that resonate with you. For example, you may want to focus on affirmations that remind you of your reasons for quitting smoking, such as "I am committed to my health and well-being," or "I am choosing a smoke-free life."

Repeat Your Affirmations: Once you've identified your affirmations, make a habit of repeating them to yourself regularly. You can say them out loud or silently to yourself, whichever feels most comfortable. Consider repeating your affirmations first thing in the morning, throughout the day, and before bed.

Visualize Your Success: As you repeat your affirmations, try to visualize yourself as a non-smoker. Imagine how you will feel when you've achieved your goal, and allow that positive feeling to fuel your motivation.

Use Affirmations to Combat Cravings: Affirmations can be particularly useful when you're experiencing cravings for cigarettes. Instead of giving in to the urge to smoke, repeat your affirmations to yourself and focus on the positive benefits of being smoke-free.

Using positive affirmations can be a simple yet effective way to stay motivated and focused on your goal of quitting smoking. Give it a try and see how it can help you in your journey to a smoke-free life.

Chapter 45: The Benefits of Drinking Water During Quitting

When you're trying to quit smoking, drinking water may not be the first thing that comes to mind. However, staying hydrated is crucial to maintaining good health and supporting your body through the quitting process. Here are some of the benefits of drinking water while you quit smoking:

It helps to flush out toxins: Smoking releases harmful chemicals into your body, which can build up over time. Drinking water can help to flush out these toxins and support your body's natural detoxification process.

It can help alleviate nicotine withdrawal symptoms: Dehydration can make nicotine withdrawal symptoms worse, such as headaches, fatigue, and irritability. By staying hydrated, you can reduce the severity of these symptoms and make the quitting process more manageable.

It promotes healthy habits: Drinking water is a healthy habit that can help replace smoking as a coping mechanism. Instead of reaching for a cigarette, try drinking a glass of water to help reduce cravings and maintain your commitment to quitting.

It supports overall health: Drinking water is essential for overall health, and it can help reduce the risk of health problems that are associated with smoking, such as heart disease, stroke, and lung cancer.

In conclusion, drinking water is an easy and effective way to support your body during the quitting process. Make sure to drink plenty of water throughout the day, and consider carrying a water bottle with you to stay hydrated on the go. By incorporating this healthy habit into your routine, you can set yourself up for success in your journey to become smoke-free.

Chapter 46: Quitting Smoking and Your Immune System

Smoking has been linked to a wide range of health problems, including an increased risk of respiratory infections, cardiovascular disease, and cancer. However, many smokers are unaware of the impact that smoking has on their immune system. In this chapter, we'll explore the ways that quitting smoking can improve your immune system.

The immune system is the body's defense against viruses, bacteria, and other harmful substances. When the immune system is functioning properly, it can identify and attack these invaders, protecting the body from illness and disease. However, smoking can compromise the immune system in a number of ways.

First, smoking can damage the lining of the respiratory tract, making it easier for viruses and bacteria to enter the body. This can increase the risk of respiratory infections such as pneumonia, bronchitis, and influenza.

Smoking can also reduce the number and function of immune cells in the body, including white blood cells, which play a critical role in fighting infections. This can weaken the immune system and make it harder for the body to fight off infections.

Fortunately, quitting smoking can help to reverse many of these negative effects on the immune system. Within just a few weeks of quitting, the body begins to repair itself. The lungs start to heal, and the risk of respiratory infections begins to decline. Over time, the number and function of immune cells in the body can also improve.

In addition to improving your immune system, quitting smoking can also help to reduce inflammation in the body. Chronic inflammation has been linked to a wide range of health problems, including cardiovascular disease, diabetes, and cancer. By reducing inflammation, quitting smoking can help to protect your overall health and well-being.

In summary, quitting smoking can have a significant positive impact on your immune system. By reducing the risk of respiratory infections, improving the function of immune cells, and reducing inflammation in the body, quitting smoking can help to improve your overall health and reduce the risk of serious illnesses and diseases.

Chapter 47: Creating a New Self-Image After Quitting Smoking

One of the most challenging aspects of quitting smoking is redefining your self-image. For many smokers, smoking is part of their identity, and quitting can leave them feeling like they have lost a part of themselves. However, quitting smoking can also be an opportunity to create a new and improved self-image.

To create a new self-image, you need to start by examining the reasons why you smoke. Is it to alleviate stress or boredom, or to fit in with a particular social group? Once you understand your reasons for smoking, you can begin to identify alternative activities and behaviors that align with your values and goals.

For example, instead of smoking during a break at work, you could take a walk around the block or listen to a favorite podcast. You could also try taking up a new hobby or exercise routine that makes you feel good about yourself and your health.

Creating a new self-image after quitting smoking also involves changing the way you think about yourself. Instead of seeing yourself as a smoker who is trying to quit, start viewing yourself as a non-smoker. Focus on the positive changes you've made and the benefits you're experiencing from not smoking, such as better health, increased energy, and improved sense of taste and smell.

Incorporating positive affirmations into your daily routine can also help to reinforce your new self-image. Repeat statements to yourself like "I am a non-smoker" and "I am committed to my health and well-being." This can help you to shift your mindset and begin to identify more fully with your new identity as a non-smoker.

Remember, quitting smoking is not just about breaking a physical addiction; it's about creating a new and healthier way of life. By embracing a new self-image and focusing on the positive changes that come with quitting smoking, you can improve your overall health and well-being for years to come.

Chapter 48: The Benefits of Deep Breathing Exercises

Deep breathing exercises are a powerful tool for managing stress and reducing cravings when trying to quit smoking. When you quit smoking, your body experiences withdrawal symptoms, which can cause anxiety and stress. Deep breathing exercises help to manage these symptoms by increasing oxygen flow to the brain and body, slowing down your heart rate and promoting relaxation.

In addition to helping with nicotine withdrawal, deep breathing exercises have a host of other benefits. They can improve lung function, boost the immune system, and reduce inflammation in the body. They can also help to lower blood pressure, decrease muscle tension, and improve overall mood and well-being.

To incorporate deep breathing exercises into your daily routine, find a quiet space where you can sit comfortably and focus on your breathing. Take a deep breath in through your nose, hold it for a few seconds, and then slowly exhale through your mouth. Repeat this process for several minutes, focusing on your breath and letting go of any distractions.

Incorporating deep breathing exercises into your quit smoking plan can help you manage cravings and stress, improve your overall health, and promote a sense of calm and well-being. Consider adding these exercises to your daily routine to support your journey to a smoke-free life.

Chapter 49: The Importance of Self-Care During Quitting

When quitting smoking, it's important to prioritize your physical and mental health. One way to do this is by practicing self-care. Self-care refers to any activities or practices that help you take care of yourself and prioritize your well-being. Here are some self-care practices that can be helpful during the quitting process:

Exercise: Exercise is an excellent way to reduce stress, improve mood, and boost overall health. Regular exercise can also help alleviate some of the physical symptoms of nicotine withdrawal, such as headaches and fatigue.

Eat a balanced diet: Eating a healthy, balanced diet can help support your body's healing process during the quitting process. Make sure to eat plenty of fruits, vegetables, lean proteins, and whole grains.

Get enough rest: Nicotine withdrawal can disrupt sleep patterns, so it's important to prioritize getting enough rest. Try to stick to a consistent sleep schedule and practice good sleep hygiene, such as avoiding screens before bed.

Practice relaxation techniques: Relaxation techniques, such as deep breathing, meditation, or yoga, can help reduce stress and promote a sense of calm. Try incorporating these techniques into your daily routine.

Treat yourself: Quitting smoking can be challenging, so it's important to celebrate your progress and reward yourself for your efforts. Treat yourself to something you enjoy, such as a favorite meal, a movie, or a massage.

By practicing self-care, you'll not only support your quitting journey but also improve your overall health and well-being. Remember, quitting smoking is a process, and it's important to be patient and kind to yourself along the way.

Chapter 50: The Power of Visualization in Quitting Smoking

Visualization is a powerful technique that can be used to support the process of quitting smoking. This technique involves creating a mental image of yourself as a non-smoker, and repeatedly visualizing this image in your mind. By doing so, you are training your brain to associate positive feelings and behaviors with being a non-smoker.

When using visualization, it is important to be specific and detailed in the mental image you create. Imagine yourself in situations where you used to smoke, but now you do not. Visualize yourself feeling confident, healthy, and in control of your life. See yourself enjoying activities that were previously difficult or unpleasant due to smoking, such as exercising or spending time with loved ones.

It can also be helpful to visualize the negative consequences of smoking, such as the impact it has on your health, relationships, and finances. By doing so, you can strengthen your motivation to quit and remind yourself of the reasons why you started this journey in the first place.

Incorporating visualization into your daily routine can be a simple but powerful tool for quitting smoking. Try setting aside a few minutes each day to visualize yourself as a non-smoker, and notice how it makes you feel. With practice, you may find that your mental image of yourself as a non-smoker becomes more vivid and realistic, making it easier to stay committed to your goal of quitting smoking for good.

Chapter 51: The Role of Accountability in Quitting Smoking

Quitting smoking is a difficult journey, and it can be helpful to have a support system in place to keep you on track. Accountability is an essential component of this support system, as it involves taking responsibility for your actions and having others hold you accountable for meeting your goals.

One way to incorporate accountability into your quitting plan is to enlist the help of a friend or family member. Tell them about your goal to quit smoking and ask them to hold you accountable for your progress. This person can check in with you regularly, offer words of encouragement, and help you stay motivated throughout the quitting process.

Another way to add accountability is to join a support group for people who are trying to quit smoking. These groups often provide a safe space for individuals to share their experiences, offer advice, and hold each other accountable for meeting their goals.

In addition to external sources of accountability, it's important to hold yourself accountable for your progress. Set clear and realistic goals for yourself, and track your progress towards these goals over time. Celebrate your successes along the way, and be honest with yourself when you experience setbacks. Remember, quitting smoking is a journey, and it's okay to stumble along the way.

Overall, accountability is a powerful tool in the quitting process. By having a support system in place and holding yourself accountable for your progress, you can increase your chances of successfully quitting smoking and living a healthier, smoke-free life.

Chapter 52: Creating a Plan for Life After Quitting Smoking

Quitting smoking is a significant accomplishment, but it's essential to have a plan for maintaining a smoke-free lifestyle in the long term. Here are some steps you can take to create a plan for life after quitting smoking:

Identify your triggers: One of the most important steps in creating a plan for life after quitting smoking is to identify your triggers. Triggers are situations, people, or events that make you want to smoke. Common triggers include stress, boredom, and social situations. By identifying your triggers, you can develop strategies to avoid or manage them.

Set goals: Setting goals is a powerful tool for maintaining a smoke-free lifestyle. Start by setting short-term goals, such as staying smoke-free for a week, and gradually work your way up to longer-term goals, such as staying smoke-free for a year. Celebrate your accomplishments along the way and use them as motivation to continue.

Develop healthy habits: Creating healthy habits can help you maintain a smoke-free lifestyle. This can include regular exercise, eating a balanced diet, and practicing stress-reducing techniques such as yoga or meditation.

Seek support: Quitting smoking is a challenging process, and having a support system can make a significant difference. Consider joining a support group, working with a therapist, or talking to friends and family members who have gone through the same process.

Plan for relapse: Relapse is a common part of the quitting process, but it doesn't have to be a setback. Plan ahead for the possibility of relapse by identifying what you'll do if you slip up, such as reaching out to your support system or revisiting your goals.

By following these steps, you can create a plan for life after quitting smoking that will help you maintain a smoke-free lifestyle and enjoy the benefits of improved health and well-being.

Conclusion

Congratulations on completing this book about quitting

smoking! By now, you should have a better understanding of the risks of smoking, the benefits of quitting, and the strategies you can use to overcome nicotine addiction.

Quitting smoking is a challenging process, and it's normal to experience setbacks along the way. Remember that quitting smoking is a journey, and it's essential to be patient and kind to yourself throughout the process.

As you move forward in your journey to quit smoking, remember to use the tools and strategies that work best for you. Whether it's mindfulness techniques, exercise, or medication, find the approaches that help you manage cravings and stay motivated.

Finally, know that you are not alone. There are countless resources and support networks available to help you quit smoking, including friends and family, healthcare professionals, and addiction specialists.

Quitting smoking is one of the most significant steps you can take to improve your health and wellbeing. By quitting smoking, you're not only improving your own life but also setting a positive example for those around you.

Thank you for taking the time to read this book, and I wish you all the best in your journey to quit smoking.

www.ingramcontent.com/pod-product-compliance
Lightning Source LLC
Chambersburg PA
CBHW061555250726
48657CB00021B/1858